'TWAS ANOTHER PROPER JOB

First published in 2021

A CIP catalogue record for this book is available from the British Library.

ISBN: 978 0 86183 355 9

RYELANDS
Halsgrove House, Ryelands Business Park,
Bagley Road, Wellington,
Somerset TA21 9PZ
Tel: 01823 653777
Fax: 01823 216796
email: sales@halsgrove.com

Part of the Halsgrove group of companies.
Information on all Halsgrove titles is available at: www.halsgrove.com

Printed and bound in India by Parksons Graphics

'TWAS ANOTHER PROPER JOB

JOHN GREENSLADE

ryelands

FOREWORD

Farmer John was persuaded to write a second book on his life and work on the farm since 2010.

He had written and planned this book, but was sadly taken before he had the chance to see it through the press. His family have been delighted to complete his work so that publication can take place and his story be told to the end.

As you will read and see, several significant things have occurred in the last ten years. My many friends and family were persistent that I tell it in print and photographs.

Conservation work is coming to fruition here on the farm, while I was honoured with an MBE for my work and my twenty-odd years on Radio Devon promoting it here in Devon. I feel the honour is shared with many others who have contributed along the way. As you will see we have had setbacks but, like many farmers, we have shown resilience while following my motto "To leave whatever we do in life a little better than we found it"!

Thanks must go to those people who have made this book possible and more interesting to readers. First to those who converted my scribble into print and type the written word, namely Sally, Wendy, Jess, Janet, and Kirsty with most of the beautiful photography by Joe Ashworth – THANK YOU ONE AND ALL. To my sister Margaret, for some enjoyable poetry again and her research into Family History. Thanks to my wife, Janette (Jan), for her support and help for more than fifty years; also my doctor for giving me the right medication over many years and my chiropractor for curing my aches and pains!

I hope you find that the last ten years of my life with conservation on the farm worth recording.

CONTENTS

CHAPTER 1

WAY FARM AND THE HISTORY OF OUR EARLY LIFE

Way Farm is situated in the Parish of Thorverton in the beautiful Exe Valley between Exmoor and Exeter. It has a red clay soil, with undulating land with not one level field on the farm when I grew up in the 1940s. Although in Thorverton parish, most of the land overlooks the beautiful village of Bickleigh and after a more recent purchase of land from the Bickleigh Estate in 1972, some of our farm borders the River Exe. History shows us that in the Assize Rolls of 1306 it was called "Atteweye". In 1782 in the land tax assessments, Way and Woodwalls were owned by Sir John Davey and farmed by Charles Paige and son Robert until 1805. Research in the Devon Records Office shows that at this time it was a farm of 82 acres, called Way, Combhay and Spireaux. The maps that came with the tenancy agreement when my father took on from the Fursdon Estate at Cadbury, show the names of fields which I still use today. Woodwalls was let in previous years as a separate farm, some 37 acres with seven fields, five of which were orchards! This included two fields called Hither and Yonder Down. The Fursdon family became owners of the estate in 1832, whose descendants still live there today with David Fursdon the present Lord Lieutenant of Devon. Names of fields in those days were more important compared with today's Ordnance Survey numbers. It is interesting that the names of the fields on the farm e.g. Pondsclose and Dryclose were called Higher and Lower Horfe (this is the old spelling for horse). Many other field names are similar as today, and I feel should be retained for historical purposes. Many names are lost when farms are sold and split up.

The Fursdon family did own many other local farms as well as Way. When my grandfather came here as a tenant in 1916, John Trolley Greenslade had been a tenant at Higher Chapletown in Cadbury, a farm of 34 acres. Frank Butt and his wife farmed Way from 1891. Frank died tragically, after being bitten by a horse! His wife farmed on alone until my grandfather came to Way.

My father was six years old when they came here during World War I and farming was a hard way to make a living. Sadly, Polly my dad's mother died in 1924, of a massive heart attack, so life was even more difficult. Whilst in Cullompton in the 1990s I was fortunate to meet Manny Elston who was in a nursing home there. He wanted to meet me, as he had worked for my grandparents at Way. He vividly described the day that Polly died. They had slaughtered a pig that day, and Gran always went to bed at nine pm, while Grandad went at ten. He found her in a serious condition and asked Manny to get a horse from Way Mead and ride to Tiverton to get a Doctor. He told me at the time it was raining "cats and dogs" and the horse was difficult to catch. Eventually off he went, and at Bickleigh Castle the river was in flood in the road. At Tiverton he forgot to warn the doctor that the river was flooded at the Castle. When he got back there the doctor's car was stuck in the water. By the time he reached the farm, Polly had died. Manny said that he was very fond of her. He also recalled how he used to take the horse and cart to Woodwalls orchard to spend the day picking Bramley apples. The cart had iron wheels and no springs and it is hard to understand how the apples did not bruise on their rough journey to Bickleigh railway station! If only I had met Manny earlier I would have learnt so much more about life here on the farm. Sadly he passed away after my second visit to him.

Interestingly I found the wages book for 1935 showing P. Connibear earned one pound twelve shillings a week. Also, at the time up to seven neighbouring farmers brought cows to our Devon bull being charged six shillings a time! From grandfather's movement book it shows that they took cattle, sheep, and pigs to Bickleigh Market until 1949, with my family winning a cup for store cattle in the 1930s. In 1939 my father

The River Exe by the lower field.

married Marjorie Isaac from Butterleigh, taking on Way tenancy at Lady Day at a rent of one hundred and sixty pounds. My father's diary shows he paid worker Mr G. Howe one pound fifteen shillings a week! How did they live on that in 1939? My history began in 1940. As a baby I was a very fussy eater but with the help of a neighbour I survived my early childhood! Sister Margaret arrived in 1945 and times were tough during and after the Second World War. We are both able to remember being brought up in a supportive family.

In 2005 we semi-retired into our new bungalow here close to the Way Farmhouse, having sold the house but retaining most of the land. We had stopped keeping cattle and sheep a few years earlier, and had planted several acres of broadleaf woodland which you will learn more about in following chapters. We then changed the farm name to Byway Farm to continue our conservation work.

THE GREENSLADE FAMILY TREE

You'll be amazed and even aghast
At our family's stories and history past
Forget about fiction and magical powers
This is real history — this is OURS!

For 400 years as we turn back the clock
We find Greenslade hailed from
farming stock
The early records are a bit hit and miss
But the detail of our forebears, I believe
is this —

In 1718, as you can see
Wed by license was Abraham G
Worlington his home, Eleanor his wife
With 7 children in their married life.

Next in descent was Abraham, his son
He being a blacksmith from Worlington
Three Crosses his home but now all to see
Is his name on a crossroads beside the odd tree.

Down another generation and
what do we see
The third chap in line, name
of Abraham G
In the parish records him we
have tracked
He married (Dorothy Turner), we know for a fact.

Their 2nd son John married Ann in 1822
They had just one child, thankfully a son
So via Charles the family tree grows
Living at Thelbridge, as far as we know.

The next generation had sons — just two
A quite small family for those times,
it's true!
John was the elder, and William
his brother
Charles their father and Mary,
their mother.

William was born in 1848
He married a widow — for children
too late!
He worked on the roads, of that
we're sure,
But further details? — we know no more!

Of great grandfather, John, we know a lot
I could write a book — but how long
have I got?
At Thelbridge in 1846, he was hatched
To the lovely Elizabeth Tolley
he was matched

John Tolley G, their first born, a boy
Born at Cypress House, Witheridge, I'm
sure was a joy?

*Three daughters followed, one
after another
To complete the family, and join
their brother*

*Then in 1884, tragedy struck
Elizabeth died of pneumonia – such
bad luck
Losing their mother at their young age
Let's turn our history over a page*

*The next thing we know – John
married again
Harriet Kingdon was her name
Pregnant when married – fancy that!
The baby arrived after two weeks flat.*

*Moving on, we know in 1888
They set out for a new life, to emigrate
To the Canadian Prairies is where
they were bound
An exciting adventure they hoped
would be found*

*John's four older children were left
with their Aunts
They were told that eventually,
given the chance
When settled in Canada, they would
be sent for
Now virtually orphans wondering
what they went for*

The children, apparently were
made to work
Treated like slaves, never to shirk
Then when they were sent for,
nobody cared
They worked for a pittance and
couldn't be spared

The four of them struggled to make
their own way
Working all hours for little or no pay
Hetta married a Murch and
Margaret a Turl
Evelyn married a Webber and that's
the three girls

Back in Manitoba, in Canada, meanwhile
It can't have been easy to make a pile!
Nine more children were born out there
Years when not pregnant, for
Harriett were rare!
In the cold hard winters, to keep the
wolf from the door
He made shoes and sold them in
a small store
Near Winnipeg, Portage La Prairie
can be found
And in Summer, he must have struggled
to work the virgin ground

Four of their children died while
still young
It must have been so sad for their Mum
To lose the babies that she bore
Would have broken her heart,
that's for sure

Meanwhile back in Devon: -
John Tolley married Mary Emma Tucker
in 1906
They moved to Way Farm, out in
the sticks
Their only child, William, born 1910
Was my Dad, and simply the nicest
of men

Farmed at Way, Dad worked with
John Tolley
And his Mum, Mary Emma, known
always as Polly
But tragedy stuck when Polly died young
Leaving a grieving husband and son,
Work was hard as Way Farm is steep
Milking cows and minding sheep
No machinery – just horse power
Nose to the grindstone, hour by hour

Dad was married in 1939
Prior to the outbreak of war was at
that time
Marjorie Isaac was the name of his wife
As they started 49 years of married life

Brother John was born in 1940
When he was young reluctant to eat
But you'd never know that that to
see him now
Six foot one, with size 11 feet!

Marg was born in 1945
To complete a family of four
With two such perfect children as us
I'm amazed they didn't have more!

Farmer John's Lament. NOT my work!

Previous History of Land, researched by the Greenslade Family

YEAR	SOURCE	PROPERTY	OWNER	OCCUPIERS
1306	Assize Rolls	"Atteweye"		
1782	Land Tax Assessments	Way, Woodwards	Sir John Davey	Charles Page valued £4.19.0
1792	L.T.A	Way, Woodwards		Charles Page
1805	L.T.A.	Way, Woodwards	Sir John Davey	Robert Page
1814	L.T.A	No mention of Way or Woodwards		
1821	L.T.A			
1832	L.T.A	Way, Woodwards	G.S Fursdon	Mrs Vinnicombe William Vinnicombe Mrs V's Brother-in-law
1841	Tithe Map	Way, Woodwards and Prowses 154 acres in all	Harriet Fursdon	William Wippell
1851	Census	Way		William Cornish Wife and daughter
1861	No mention of Way or Woodwards, probably uninhabited at the time.			
1871	Census	Way Farmhouse		John Phillips (widower) with 8 teenage children
1878	White's Directory	Way		William Phillips
1881	Census	Way		John Phillips (52 years old) Farmer 200 acres 2 daughters, 3 sons
1891	Census	Way		Frank Butt Wife and daughter
1893	Kelly's Directory	Way		George Butt
1916	Family knowledge	Way, Woodwards, and Prowses	Fursdons	John Trolley Greenslade Wife and son aged six
1939	Family Knowledge	Way, Woodwards and Prowses	Fursdons	William Greenslade and wife
1950	Family Owned	Way, Woodwards and Prowses	Farm bought by William Greenslade from Fursdon Estate for £5000	
1972	Family Owned	Way, Woodwalls and part of the castle estate. Prowses sold off	Farmed to date by John William Greenslade and Janette Greenslade	

CHAPTER 2

THE CREATION OF TWO WILDFLOWER MEADOWS, 2011

Just after I wrote *'Twas a Proper Job* in 2010 we worked hard to increase wildflowers in our two meadow areas. My great friend, Cyril Cole who has a large SSSR area on his farm at Rose Ash, encouraged us to bring back some of his varieties of orchids and other wildflowers into the herbage.

Digging out the heart-shaped pond.

New ponds from the wildflower meadow.

We cut both our two areas (tight to the ground) in late July after removing all the grass, using a vibrotiller and lightly disturbed the top turf. Cyril cut an area of his SSSR late at night and then big baled early the next morning when lots of varieties of wildflowers were in seed. He did it this way so he didn't lose too many of the seeds on a dewy night. I fetched a total of eight bales as soon as they were ready with my tractor and trailer and returned to the farm. Jan drove the tractor with a bale spike, and one at a time went to the meadow where I took off the net wrap and scattered the 'green hay' over the areas.

The areas were then rolled with a heavy roller before sheep were put in for a few days so their feet would tread in some of the seed. Cyril told us it would take a few years to fully establish.

The next early summertime we saw many wildflowers coming up, especially yellow rattle, buttercups, cuckoo flowers, ribwort plantain, red and white clover to name just a few!!

Tree planting and landscaping.

We had always seen a few heath spotted orchids in the wetter areas which came through again. Each year we cut the meadows in early August making old fashioned hay. After three or four years we began to see a good number of heath spotted and southern marsh orchids in the pasture. The yellow rattle had worked well in suppressing the modern grasses, being acidic, allowing the selection of wildflowers to come through. By 2017 there were literally hundreds of orchids and even found a greater butterfly orchid. In 2019 the whole area of one was mixed with several hundred of both varieties of orchid. Many other wildflowers became established such as birds foot trefoil.

Knapweed, ribwort, black medic, hawkweed and some sneezewort, melancholy thistle and snakes head fritillary. This exercise has been a great success whilst in the smaller dryer area we have now a good spring showing of wild daffodils with a variety of trees lining the area. Many orange tip butterflies have been seen. These areas are getting quite rare in the countryside so thank you Cyril for all your advice and help. You can now scatter with an old grass forager which makes it so much easier.

But it did not stop here, for our love of ponds gave us opportunity, again with Cyril's dowsing skills, to dig one at the bottom of Great Hill in the shape of a heart!!

The first pond we dug in 2000 has become established with many wetland flowers giving a display from early spring till autumn. We have ducks, herons, moorhens and the occasional otter visiting which I was able to catch on camera with three young cubs.

In 2016 my regular presenter Pippa Quelch was moved from a Sunday morning programme to a weekday evening slot so it was not easy for her to visit and record my monthly segment on Radio Devon. So after twenty years (one a month) this came to an end. We did have a 'live' broadcast from here on the farm when Matt Woodley and Pippa were visiting places of interest in Devon. Quite a few people came from all over the county to see the Wildflower Meadow and were spoken to on air about their visit. We have some very good feedback from the visitors, whilst many visit our nature trails and our annual charity Bluebell Walk for Children's Hospice South West.

In 2019 we took the opportunity to plant a riverside narrow strip of various wildflowers in late September. After three small floods some varieties have appeared in June – corn marigold, corn cockle with some yellow rattle and common mouse ears.

One of the mature ponds.

CHAPTER 3

DISEASE IN WOODLAND BYWAY FARM, 2013

Byway Farm Woods are located in the Exe Valley between Thorverton and Bickleigh. The woods extend to approximately 30 ha.

The land undulates steeply between a series of orientated ridges and streams, which drain into the River Exe. In the middle 90s, after a series of TB outbreaks, cattle were sold. We decided to plant mainly native broadleaf woodland. Financial help came through the FWPS (Farm Woodland Premium Scheme) and advice from FWAG (Farming & Wildlife Advisory Group) and the Silvanus Trust. The first of four phases started in 1996, with oak, ash, wild cherry, birch etc. planted in wavy lines in groups of 20 or 30. Three more phases followed, totalling in 28.5 ha.

Planting was organised to reduce obtrusiveness in the landscape at 2250 stems per ha, in the interest of producing quality stems. Shelters protected all the trees and the 10% open space allowances were used to create footpaths, while shrubs of berry-bearing fruit for birds in the winter lined the sides in spirals. We wished to retain the wildflower species and link the paths to two wildflower areas so the general public could enjoy all the orchids and wildflowers in season. Six ponds were also created over the same period.

The Objectives (including environmental, economic and social considerations) were to:

1. Actively develop the commercial potential of the timber crop within the woodland through sound silvicultural practices and optimise them consistent with other objectives (aiming initially for financial break-even as the woods emerge from establishment phase and an operating profit thereafter, whilst increasing the capital asset value of the property).

2. Introduce professional management advice to guide the development of the woodland and to provide continuity of input to family members in preparation for and during a period of succession and handover.
3. Maintain and enhance the range of biodiversity, conservation and amenity interests present on site through careful, integrated habitat management.
4. Enjoying the pleasure of owning and developing the woodland to UKFS standards.
5. Allow other people to enjoy the woodland, emphasising and providing opportunities for learning skills and where appropriate business development.

After several successful years in the Devon County Show Woodland Competition, winning the Warkins Trophy for new woodland management under twenty years again for the third and fourth time in 2010 and 2013 was very satisfying.

We also won the Stuckley Cup for establishment and care in 2011, 2015 and 2017; again we have been proud of our achievements over several years.

BUT in 2013 came our "Covid 19 experience".

For over thirty years I have been a scorer at many of the South West shearing competitions and spent four days regularly at the Bath and West Show at Shepton Mallet in Somerset. I enjoy taking my quad bike around the woodland two or three times a week and returning from the show I did my usual trip on a Monday morning in early June. It was noticeable that the six-year-old ash was not sprouting any leaves on the top third of many of the young trees (about 80%). I became quite concerned as Ash Dieback was already in Eastern counties. I thought it was wise to contact the Forestry Commission and the supplier of the whips (in Somerset). The supplier took samples and assured me it was not Ash Dieback but would send samples for testing. The Forestry Commission advice was to put your concerns on 'Tree Alert'. Nothing happened for a few days but my tractor mechanic who was doing a repair for me told me his partner worked for the Forestry Commission.

Fruiting bodies.

Together we went and looked at the infected trees and he phoned his partner after which we were visited by the head of the Forestry Commission Research, Ben and the supplier of the original whips.

They went and took samples of several young ash trees and did DNA tests on our kitchen table! The results were devastating and Ben's words were "that is was not thought possible that Ash Dieback had reached the West Counties". On further inspection by the Research team, the disease was found in several of our field plantations.

We were issued with a Movement Restriction notice with RED no entry signs on all our road gates which felt like the Foot and Mouth restrictions a few years earlier. We were then asked to dig up and burn all the young ash trees (1500) in twenty-four hours to avoid spread to neighbouring woodland.

Diamond lesions.

The spore catcher.

Burning young ash trees.

A team of helpers plus two mini diggers and quad and trailer worked tirelessly through the day and completed the tasks within twenty-four hours. Firstly the plastic tubes and stakes had to be removed, following on with diggers and picking up teams.

We were told we were the first major outbreak in the South West, so inevitably the press and TV became involved and it made headline news. BBC reporters and camera crew spent all day at our site, followed by ITV for three hours the following day.

As you can imagine we were in shock for a while but the research team were very comforting, saying "we cannot be blamed for this outbreak".

After a few weeks of research is was revealed that the ash whips had been grown in Belgium. The seed was bought in Germany who sold it on to Belgium with no border restrictions!

For several months nothing could be moved off site but in October we were granted some funding towards the cost of replanting. This time a group of children (thirteen-sixteen years) with learning difficulties plus volunteers planted, tubed and staked a fresh selection of young whips.

They were – wild cherry, hornbeam, lime, whitebeam and a dozen wild service (quite rare and expensive!)

The young helpers worked really hard and their carers said they had never seen them so happy, being outside their classrooms! Not using mobile phones!

The fungal disease is mostly spread by wind and birds and can travel several miles. The spores could be found on the branches of leaves lying on the ground in warm weather brachts. Not all ash trees succumb to the disease and we were contacted by the Food and Environment Research Agency asking if they could place some spore traps in areas of the older ash trees (sixteen years) where the disease was noticeable. These traps (see photo) were operated by a 12-volt battery. Every week we had to change the sticky tape, recharge the battery, and then send the reels back to York University to compute the number of spores. This continued until the autumn. In 2014 they brought a single spore catcher and rain water containers which we maintained until September.

Young ash tree affected by the disease.

As the disease became more apparent in the trees we were asked by Ben if we could not fell about 100 trees in one area of woodland so they could monitor at various times. In the summer the Forestry Commission flew a helicopter over our woods taking pictures which made it easy to see how Ash Dieback had taken its toll. The disease was becoming more noticeable in the local woods and hedges in the locality. We were asked by Bob of Devon County Council Highways if he could bring colleagues from the Roads Department, so they could then identify any roadside trees that had been infected and becoming dangerous.

On one occasion we had more than 30 DCC vans parked in our top yard, but they were good in disinfecting their boots!

In 2016 Ben asked if there were any ash keys on any of the 100 trees left in that one area, not showing signs of infection?

We found two with keys and in late autumn, Mike (Ben's Deputy) came and collected two large bags of keys which were going to be grown in the research labs to see if they had a good resistance to Ash Dieback.

After 2014 we hired contractors to fell many of the infected trees in two groups of woodland where the wood could only be used as firewood. Nick Downie firstly bought a firewood processor which cut the long logs into fire length and then split them into usable sizes. Nick then bought a tree harvester which is a fantastic bit of machinery which can grab a tree, cut it close to the ground, strip the branches, cut to required length and stack in suitable piles. Being mechanically trained he soon was using it in other parts of our woodland, thinning as well as taking down the diseased ash. In all to date he has probably felled well over 12,000 trees! To get the trees out he had to create and widen paths so that tractor and timber trailers could travel easily and safely.

Around 2015 we had a call from a young lady from Yorkshire who was visiting her mother in Seaton and had heard of the problems here with Ash Dieback and she asked if she could visit and see our woodland. We found out she was an author who had written several books. She is called Lisa Samson and wanted to write a book entitled 'Epitaph for the Ash'. The inspiration had come from her late uncle who had written a book 'Epitaph for the Elm'. After recording for two-three hours she said she would like to do more in a years' time. In about eighteen months' time she made contact again apologising for the delay. Driven here by her husband she was still determined to finish her book and she sent me a copy of the chapter on this farm's experience to read and then in time sent the book in the post, she had finished. I recommend it to any readers.

There are contrasts with the Ash Dieback disease and the Covid 19 pandemic that we are experiencing now.

The older trees, of which I mean 100 years still caught the disease but took longer to succumb fully to the virus whereas the young saplings show very early signs, perhaps two-three years old. This is the opposite in most case to the Covid 19 disease in humans.

In the earlier times with Dutch Elm Disease, young trees in the hedgerows grew to about 15-20 feet before the beetle attacked and killed them which can be seen here in the Exe Valley.

When Nick (our contractor) took down numerous groups of infected trees, which had been mostly planted fifteen-thirty years before, in groups of 30-50, he left any ash that showed no signs of Ash Dieback. This was probably 10% but in the succeeding years half of these became infected and it is evident that any ash seeds that are to be seen underneath the canopy are becoming infected very quickly. We were a little disappointed that a few individuals, over the last few years blame us for bringing Ash Dieback to the South West, but we were comforted by Ben and his team that at some stage it would have reached the South West, as it was already rampant in the Eastern areas.

There seem to be ever increasing threats to our countryside from livestock and woodland disease affecting and challenging our farming and forestry industry. In the livestock sector we have to face up to Foot and Mouth, TB, Blue Tongue, Mad Cow Disease, Fowl Pest, to name but a few and there are other ones in the forestry sector challenging us at the moment i.e. oak decline moth, chestnut blight and ash borer beetle which have killed many thousands in the USA and Canada.

So farmers and foresters face ever more of a fight to maintain our livestock and forestry sectors. Let us hope we can keep any more diseases under control in the United Kingdom.

CHAPTER 4

PROUD TO BE MID DEVON SHOW PRESIDENT, 2013

In my previous book I told how a group of us, led by Roger Hill, agreed to bring back a show in Mid Devon on the 4th Saturday in July. I was the first Show Director in 1994 at Hartnoll Farm, Post Hill, Tiverton.

From humble beginnings, "the Oak planted that year" has grown into quite a large tree. It made me proud to have been part of the team since its inauguration and in 2012 it was voted "The Best One Day Show" in the country in the *Farmers Guardian* competition.

But, I was even prouder to have been asked to be the President in 2013, the 20th show, leading a splendid team of volunteers who work tirelessly for the previous two weeks on site for a crowd of around 15,000. Then a further ten days clearing the site so it could return to Agriculture use.

Of course there had been many hours of committee meetings putting together plans for show day, which was a day to remember with Jan

Proud to be Show President.

presenting trophies to winners in the main ring. Jan had been involved for several years in the children's painting competition which attracts several hundred entries displayed in the Food Hall.

The livestock at Mid Devon Show are some of the best presented at any of the shows in the West Country. Many rural crafts are demonstrated each year and some of the best local food producers sell their produce here.

Vintage tractors and machinery are there with some of them showing how it used to be done in years gone by. Mid Devon has prided itself for being

Outside the Children's Hospice South West Stand.

one that has a demonstration area where visitors can see new and old tractors and machinery perform their tasks. Many of the machinery businesses provide hospitality at their stands. The main ring gives the public a huge variety of entertainment from Young Farmers to motorbike displays and of course the main ring livestock parade where winners are on display to one and all.

One section I always enjoy watching are the Heavy Horses with some of their brass and other decorations. We have, I am told, one of if not the best displays in a one day show in the South West. Another tent worth visiting is the flower tent with its magical displays now run very efficiently by Brenda Tucker. After the move to the new showground at Knightshayes in 2015, where more space was available, the marquee was well placed to show Mid Devon off in flowers. In 2018 and 2019 Jan became a steward and she painted scenery for "The Wizard of Oz" which won 1st prize in its class. 2019 saw Jan paint the scenery for "Here Comes the Sun" and came 2nd in its class. She painted four beach huts to front the marquee.

In recent years my daughter and son-in law, with grandson Steven, showed some of their Holsten Friesian Cattle and we were very proud in 2017 when they won the supreme championship of the show with Allerways Star 38 which was a great achievement also best presented.

In the cattle section it had been difficult getting some breeders to exhibit because of the TB outbreaks in our countryside. I was asked to judge the best presented in all types of livestock, quite an honour. My views have always been, especially when we lost nearly fifty cattle back in mid 1994, that there must be a balance in nature. Too many wild animals, be it deer, fox or badgers cause health problems in all the livestock areas, whether it be cattle, sheep or poultry.

Taking a break during the show.

This year due to Covid 19 all the shows have had to be cancelled but let's hope that next year there will be more shows showing off the Devon countryside to one and all.

Finally to be President of Mid Devon Show was an honour and a privilege and thank you to organisers and voluntary stewards that yearly give so much time to keep the show on the road.

Daughter and son-in-law – the Allerways Herd.

In the Orchard.

CHAPTER 5

PLANTING A DEVON APPLE ORCHARD, 2015

In my childhood my father, and previously my grandfather, made cider for themselves and the workers from an old cider press in Way barn. At that time, we probably had four areas of orchard around the farmhouse and a bramley orchard at Woodwalls. Cider was certainly needed at harvest and threshing times. A gentleman who worked for my grandfather was called Manny Elston. As I have said earlier, I met him in a nursing home in Cullompton in the early 1990s after a fellow magistrate on the Bench told me that he was keen to meet me. Although he was rather poorly, he related to me on two occasions his memories of work at the farm. He told me about me about the day my grandmother died, when he rode a horse to Tiverton to fetch a doctor. Interestingly he told how he took a horse and cart (on steel wheels) to the bramley orchard at Woodwalls. There he would first pick up a cart load of apples put in boxes and take them to Bickleigh Station where they were loaded on a train to London. Sadly, the poor man died before I could learn more of his time on the farm. In later years we took our cider apples to Whiteways in Whimple, Horrels in Stoke Canon and Inch's in Winkleigh.

After we moved here into the bungalow in 2005 we made a new vegetable garden on the top of Great Hill. This worked well in the first few years but after a while roe deer and rabbits enjoyed our peas, kidney beans and lettuce quicker than we did! Then came about the idea of giving up the vegetable garden and planting this area to old varieties of Devon apples. We found a supplier of young apple trees in Payhembury in 2015 and with the help of a couple of contractors and family (and a mini digger) planted them on a late December day. Twelve varieties of cider, twelve cookers and twelve desserts and crab apples. The table with their names is shown below, some of which have a local connection. On the 15th January – Wassail Day – we all celebrated with cider, banging dustbin lids and singing suitable songs.

DEVON APPLE ORCHARD 2015

COOKERS	EATERS	CIDER
Peter Lock	Limberland	Killerton Sharp
Woolbrook Russet	Star of Devon	Browns
Whimple Wonder	Exeter Cross	Sweet Alford
Cherry Surprise	Luccombe Pine	Fairmaid of Devon
Farmers Glory	Tom Putt	Payhembury
Upton Pyne	Devonshire Quarrenden	Tale Sweet
Pigs Nose	Red Sentinel (crab)	Court Royal
English Codling	Sops In Wine	Black Dabinet
Ashmeads Kernel	Plumb Vite	Sweet Coppin
Fortune	Tregonna King	Ellis Bitter
Elstar	Slack Me Girdle	Kirton Fair
	Lord Lamborne	Major
	Plympton Pippen	Tremletts Bitter

Planting the apple orchard.

The orchard has developed well and in 2019 there was an excellent crop of many apples. We have put plastic name signs beneath each tree whilst calling it Manny Elston's Orchard.

Apples.

Inspecting the apples.

CHAPTER 6

A MIGHTY BIG EXPERIENCE, 2017

On the 21st November 2016, there came through the post a letter from the Cabinet Office. My first thoughts were that, as a retired magistrate, I still can witness and give references to some special documents when asked to do so. I am on the supplementary list, but not sitting in court. We were told to ask the court office if we were not sure if we could do so in certain cases. I had, a couple of weeks before, confirmed the nationality of someone I had personally known for well over twenty-five years and did not see a problem in this instance. So, my first thoughts were that I had made a mistake in confirming my friend's nationality. On opening the letter, with some apprehension, I nearly fell off my chair when the first line read "The Prime Minister, after advice from the Main Honours Committee, proposes to submit your name to the Queen, to be appointed a Member of the British Empire (MBE) in the 2017 New Year's Honours List". I had to agree to this proposal and the Honours List would be published on 31st December in the *London Gazette*. This letter made clear it was in strict confidence, so for the next six weeks, we could tell no one of this coming honour for services to Agricultural Education and Conservation in the West Country. The investiture at Buckingham Palace would be held in the next seven months.

It became very difficult to keep it from our family and friends and to say how proud I was at this news. Just before Christmas, a lady from the Cabinet Office rang me to confirm the details that the nominees who had put my name forward for an award had supplied were correct before they were released to the press. It was not long before some reporters were in contact for an interview. By this time the news of my impending

Proud to be presented my MBE by Prince Charles.

honour was becoming really hard to keep from our three daughters and family. The official publication of the list is in the Government's "paper of record", the *London Gazette*.

Family photo.

When the news broke on New Year's Eve, the family were, I think, as shocked as I had been initially. Many phone calls and congratulatory letters and cards followed in the next couple of weeks. Many were from committee members of various organisations I had worked with over many years. One of the first to arrive was from the Permanent Secretary of DEFRA, although I had not worked on any of their committees! Others came from the Chair of Mid Devon District Council and one from the Lord Lieutenant of Devon, David Fursdon, whose predecessors were landlords of Way Farm when my grandfather came to the farm in 1916. After receiving all the marvellous cards and letters, I felt very proud to have worked with so many people who had supported me through the many ventures in my life. We have, over the years, supported various charities but none more so than Children's Hospice South West. One of the aims of our conservation work on the farm has been to bring young people with all kinds of disabilities into the countryside. Annually, we have held walks for many different organisations, including the Women's Institute, walking for health groups and many others – too many to mention!

My wife, Janette and my two eldest daughters, Sally and Wendy, were the three guests that I was allowed to take to the Palace. We were told the date (19th May) about six weeks prior to the ceremony and the ladies then spent valuable time finding suitable finery for the special day in May. As for me and my attire, I normally hate shopping but luckily, I had only bought a new suit a few months previously for my grandson's wedding, so all that was left to do was to source a shirt and tie. I had, at a Devon Young Farmers event, met the Lord Lieutenant of Devon, who encouraged me to wear a tie that represented what I had won the MBE for. So, I went online to look for one with wildflowers on. After a couple of hours online, the wife and I found one that looked ideal and with a couple of clicks on the computer, the order was placed. Three days later, both the white shirt and the tie arrived. After a fitting, the shirt and tie looked the part, so there was my attire ready for London.

We decided to book a hotel in London in the Waterloo area for the day before, not too far from the Palace by taxi. The train journey was booked online from Honiton station. Neither I or Janette had been on a train journey for years but we managed to get a four-seat section with table, allowing plenty of room for the hat box and all the ladies attire to travel safely to London! Our son-in-law, Richard, took us to the station where South West trains were right on time. The journey took us through some varied countryside with various stock and crops. At Waterloo, we had our first 'taste' of busy London. A row of taxis, as far as we could see, were in line to take passengers to their destinations, including ours to the hotel.

On our arrival to London, we were greeted by heavy rain, which continued to pour as we journeyed through many traffic jams to our hotel by taxi. At the hotel, we found our booked rooms, which we were all pleased with. The decision was taken to visit and eat at Fortnum and

Mason in the Gallery restaurant. This business was established in 1707 and boy was it a store, like nothing I had been in before! We ordered fish and chips with split peas. This was the dearest fish and chips I have ever had but it was superbly cooked and presented, well worth the money. The ladies spent some time, after the meal, viewing the very elaborate and expensive goods on display. Many tourists were buying goods and hampers of first-class products. Leaving Fortnum and Mason, the rain was still pouring down, so we hailed a taxi back through London and its wonderful tourist attractions, to the hotel for the evening.

Early to bed and early to rise for breakfast at 7 am, heartily enjoyed before back to our rooms to put on all our finery. The weather was as forecast with cloud, but no rain. We left our cases in a safe area in the hotel and the taxi arrived at 9 am. We were told to arrive at the South Centre Gate to the Palace, which our driver had not encountered before, so with the many road works taking place outside the Palace, he lost his way in. After police advice, we walked the last 100 yards! At the gates, we produced our passes and photo ID, then waited in line for ten minutes before entering the Palace through the Quadrangle. Once inside, we were parted, guests to the left into the Grand Ballroom and myself directed to another room where eventually the ninety or so recipients mingled with each other for about an hour. At 10.40 am, the Lord Chamberlain, dressed in his spurs, took us through the procedure on receiving our medals from Prince Charles. There were two huge screens in the Gallery which we could follow as the ceremony proceeded. Shortly before 11.00am, one of the officials from the Lord Chamberlain's office called out the medalists in programme order in groups of around fifteen people. I was in the next to last group to be called forward. On arriving at the side Gallery, we could view the most elaborate paintings of previous special occasions in years past at the Palace. The moment had finally arrived for my name to be announced and for me to present myself to the dais and Prince Charles. As I stood there, next in line, I noticed my family were sitting in the very front row of seats! Following the procedure of standing 2 yards from the Prince, I bowed my head then approached His Royal Highness, who clipped the MBE medal to my lapel. We conversed for a couple of minutes and then, shaking my hand, I reversed 2 yards, bowed then left by the other side door. The medal was unclipped, boxed with numerous congratulations by Palace staff as I made my way to the seats at the back of the Ballroom. All through the ceremony, the Countess of Wessex's String Orchestra played wonderfully suitable music. The splendour of the Palace has to be seen to be believed!

After the final presentations and the National Anthem, the Prince left the Ballroom with the entourage from the dais. There were two Gurkhas, five Yeomen of the Guard and his various equerries. My ladies were honoured to be sitting in the front row seats, although this resulted in them having to be the last ones to leave the Ballroom and thus it took some time for them to join me for the official photos taken in the Quadrangle. Thankfully, the weather continued to be dry with brief glimpses of sunshine. The ladies had to recover their bags and cameras from a cloakroom where their belongings were returned in a gold carrier bag with coat of arms! They were amused by the wooden toilets in the cloakrooms, real Victorian antiques! After an hour's wait in the Quadrangle, it was time to have the official photos taken. We were not allowed to take our own photos with any Palace door in the background.

With all the necessary photos taken, it was time to go back to the hotel, change and taxi back to Waterloo Station to catch the 3.20pm train to Honiton. We did have a few showers between Andover and Sherborne, but back in East Devon, it had remained dry. As we neared home, we decided to have a meal together at a local pub, which was enjoyed by all. What a day!!

The next day, many friends and relations were enquiring about the experience. All I can say is how proud I was of my family at sharing this around. I would like to thank those who put forward my name for an award, it is a truly wonderful experience. Mostly, a grateful thank you to the Young Farmers Movement. Without their training in my time as a Member and beyond would I have achieved so much in life? I never for one moment thought I would receive such a prestigious award. I feel the honour must be shared with all those people in the various organisations I have been involved with over the last sixty or seventy years. What a Mighty Big Experience!

CHAPTER 7

HEALTH EXPERIENCES, CELLULITIS AND ANKLE FUSIONS, 2016-18

July 2016 – I have always enjoyed watching the André Rieu concerts on television, especially the ones from his own town of Maastricht in Holland. An opportunity arose to enjoy live, one of his concerts when Blakes Tours did a few day trips in early July. We left early on a Friday morning, by coach to Dover for the crossing to Calais. A smooth crossing and after crossing France, Belgium arrived at our hotel in Valkenburg at 7pm. The evening meal was not ready on arrival but at 8pm in the middle of a rather basic meal I felt unwell and went up to our bedroom. When Jan came up, I was sweating profusely, and she noticed my left leg was red, hot, and inflamed.

After an uncomfortable night we enquired if there was a pharmacy near, but being a Saturday, they did not open until 11am. The Blakes Tours had fixed a trip into Germany to a tourist town of Monschau with a 10am start. The driver said there would probably be a pharmacy there but on arrival he gave us his mobile number if we could not get any help. Jan made a few enquiries, but most people only spoke German, however a kind German who spoke good English told us there was no pharmacy in Monschau. A phone call to the driver told us to meet him at the tourist centre at the bottom of the town. Walking was fairly painful but at the tourist centre they said there was a pharmacy 8km in a nearby village. After a walk on cobbled streets to the bus stop, Graham (the bus driver) took us and we saw a German pharmacist, who taking one look at my leg said you must see a doctor urgently. The doctor would be at a local hospital some 2 km away so off we went after the pharmacist had phoned the hospital to say we were on our way. The bus driver drove us to a very modern hospital, booked in, waited five minutes and a nurse took all the details, passport, health card, age etc.

In another five minutes I was seen by a doctor who quickly diagnosed me as diabetic and the leg as infected with cellulitis for which antibiotics were necessary. The pharmacy was 100 metres from the hospital and after paying 200 euros I took two tablets from the box which was all written in German. I had completely forgotten to tell him I also had a bad reaction to penicillin!

Graham, then bussed us back to Monschau where after a couple of hours, we all returned to the Valkenburg Hotel. A retired 'District Nurse' on our trip advised me to keep the leg elevated, which did relieve some of the intense pain. The temperature was in the 80s so after another uncomfortable night. I was determined after all this travel to see André Rieu's concert that started at 8pm. The concert is held in the large square in Maastricht, with many restaurants on the outside with seating for several thousand in the square itself. The set is brilliantly illuminated with large screens making for better viewing to the people at the back and side.

We arrived at 7 pm with Jan and me taking our time, with stops on the many seats on the 400 metres to the Square. The concert was starting in daylight with extraordinary artificial lighting as the show went on. We just sat back and enjoyed a truly exhilarating show with André introducing a huge variety of music, with the excellent voices of the regular guest singers. We arrived back at the hotel at 1am and straight to bed for an early start in the morning. All went well, with me resting my leg on a used seat on the bus elevated until we got back to the jungle at Calais. We waited two hours to get through customs and then one further hour for loading into the ferry. We arrived back at Byways at 1 am Tuesday.

On Mid Devon Show day, which I did not attend, I had a Facetime call from my grandson Alex and his girlfriend Emma in Canada. Emma's father is a doctor who after viewing online told me to go to hospital as soon as possible as my condition could be life threatening.

A long story ensued with me having to go the Royal Devon and Exeter Hospital every morning for an intravenous injection followed by a month of 'stomach' upsetting antibiotic tablets. But despite all this the show in Maastricht was BRILLIANT.

Jan has had a bad reflux problem which got worse, so she saw a consultant at Nuffield who referred her to one of the best in the west surgeons. After numerous unpleasant tests in December he confirmed she needed an operation and was noted urgent, hoping the operation to be in January or February. Alas after numerous phone calls to his secretary we only heard it would be on 13th May. For months she was having sleepless nights with acid in her mouth. It was confirmed that she had a hiatus hernia that might need repairing at the same time. The operation took three hours and she was on a liquid diet for six weeks after. Now in 2020 the reflux has been cured and with regular medication life is much better.

The Ankle Fusion Experience 2017

More than twenty years ago I had to undergo an ankle fusion on my left ankle after damaging it over a period of years. It was early June and I, at the time, had done no round bale silaging. The surgeon had told me it needed doing urgently, so I had little choice. I remember being in hospital several days and in plaster for ten weeks. It was just after this time I bought my first quad bike, which allowed me after a few weeks to travel around the farm. It took quite a long time to put full pressure on the ankle and so my right ankle took a great deal of pressure. Even after many months of recuperation things were no different. I had great difficulty in depressing the clutch in the car, so eventually we had to purchase an automatic car where no clutch was required. Silly little things like getting out of the bath, climbing upstairs and climbing up farm hillsides became a bit more of a challenge. But now years later, the extra work on the right ankle began to cause me problems. This had become painful when walking on hard surfaces and uneven ground.

So much so that I succumbed to the doctor arranging an x-ray at Tiverton Hospital in early April and he made an appointment to see a surgeon.

His initial response was my right ankle needed a fusion and my left an injection of steroids under x-ray guidance. At this time, wife Jan was not able to drive after being taken off the road for a suspected TIA (mini stroke). So, I opted to have both procedures under the NHS. We needed one of us to be able to drive. The appointment time would be four months (in pain). Meanwhile our retired surgeon neighbour visited and informed me not to wait but go private at the Nuffield in Exeter where "some of the best orthopaedic surgeons in the country work". So, I took his advice and arranged an appointment. Jan by this time had regained her driving licence. My appointment was on 13th August at a very busy clinic. The surgeon came to the waiting room to fetch us and after viewing the existing x-ray he suggested that he needed a further x-ray of my left foot which took place on that day. He agreed that I needed a guided injection of steroid in my left foot. My right ankle definitely needed fusing but a CT scan would help him see if more needed to be

Recovering with my faithful friend.

done during the operation. What was good was that he had a model of the foot which he could demonstrate where the problems were. None of this was seen at Tiverton Hospital and he explained he did not want me to have further trouble in a few years, as the cartilage was completely gone, it was bone on bone.

A CT scan was arranged by his secretary and two weeks later I met the surgeon for the injection and the scan.

He confirmed that the answer was key hole surgery with pins and it would be approximately four-six weeks later. I then got together all the jobs that needed doing before the operation. I was to be in plaster for six weeks, no walking on it whilst in plaster. Having been through a similar operation before, I knew it would take some time to heal six to eight months was the surgeon's estimate. The initial appointment was 20th November delayed to January. I rang and spoke to the secretary who said she would try to get it earlier. Next lunchtime she rang to ask if I could make 13th October which I readily agreed to although it was Friday 13th! I am not superstitious, but next lunchtime she rang to say that due to unforeseen circumstances it would now be the 23rd October at 7am. Pre-op assessment was twelve days before which I presume went well!

Prior to the operation I took as much time possible to prepare the tractors for winter with antifreeze. The contractor was trimming our hedges and Nick Downie, after finishing with the tree harvester, was finishing off the new tracks through the woodland. This was important so they could settle before the diseased ash in 8 foot lengths could be extracted safely.

Although a little early, Jan and I took up the young oak trees that were growing amongst her flowers and shrubs, probably buried acorns by jays or squirrels! We then replanted them in the demonstration area amongst many dead young ash trees. (The Forestry Commission Research Unit asked for this area to be left untouched.) One of the very last jobs 22/10/17 was (I thought) to cut the lawn for the last time this year, and to fully clean and oil the ride on mower.

The morning of the operation we were up at 5am with no breakfast for me, only a sip of water! Jan had put together all I needed for the overnight stay at the Nuffield Hospital in Exeter. We arrived at 6.30am and at reception were booked in and soon taken to our room (23) on the 23rd October. Within a very short time I was seen by a physiotherapist who, after taking height and weight measurements went and brought a granny hopping frame adjusted to my height. He was quickly followed by a staff nurse, who was a farmer's wife from Okehampton. She checked all my credentials and then put the named label on my wrist and bed. Checks then for temperature and blood pressure were completed. The housekeeper came with the menu for dinner and next morning's breakfast. By 8.15 am the surgeon directed black marker pens to my right ankle whilst filling out the consent form for me to sign. The anaesthetist arrived and explained his role. This included how he would inject into a nerve at the back of my leg, which would make the leg below the knee painless for at least ten to twelve hours. The pain disappeared after I signed the consent form, with the comment "see you in theatre". At 9am the nurse came to walk me to the theatre, up one floor to one of the theatres and recovery rooms. Up onto the bed and the anaesthetist went straight to work. Needle in the back of the hand in vein and soon the aesthetic worked its magic.

The operation I was told went well (three hours) and I drowsily remember seeing the clock in the recovery room, at 1.45 pm. I honestly cannot remember being wheeled back to my room. My right ankle and leg was in a temporary plaster to allow for swelling after the operation. It was important to keep the leg elevated and immobile for twenty-four hours. After the operation the nurses visited frequently to monitor my observations and pinch my toes. Some of them thinking I was a "celebrity" Farmer John on Radio Devon. The consultant visited confirming the operation went well, no complications and that the temporary plaster would remain for two weeks followed by a full plaster for a month, with no pressure on the ankle. After this in a special boot for six weeks. The following day Jan duly arrived.

After this I was given injections for daily use to avoid blood clots, pain killers and a "limbo" to use on my leg so I could safely have a bath. A ride on scooter was booked for two weeks' time and wheelchair-bound was taken to the car for my first lesson in transferring from chair to vehicle which was achieved clumsily and my journey home was completed. I was surprised at how little pain I was in and managed on paracetamol.

Although the initial operation of the wheelchair took a while to get used to, hiring from the Red Cross was very reasonable and I soon became accustomed to its versatility. Getting onto the kitchen sofa was easier than the reverse but Penny Prosser came to the rescue, a retired physiotherapist by bringing house bricks to raise the sofa by two inches. My granddaughter Jess, an occupational therapist, regularly kept an eye on me making sure I kept wriggling my toes and standing up at times. Over the next ten days I was pushed outside on sunny days. I did not want to get too "housey". I returned to the Nuffield after eleven days where the temporary plaster and stitches were removed. A new fully covered plaster enclosed my ankle and leg. Here I did meet briefly the consultant's secretary whose ancestors were related to me. The plaster was reinforced around my ankle and leg to remain for another month.

The scooter that had been recommended by the physiotherapist was hired from Taunton but to date I was struggling in getting onto it!

Jan had been able to continue with her Art and Pilates classes as I could navigate the bungalow (other than outside when I could not as yet get back in the house). One amusing experience with the wheelchair (in her absence) was that on one frosty morning she put an old bubble hat on my exposed toes for warmth. I went to the loo and because there is not too much room in the bathroom, I reversed out in the chair. The flaming hat came off the toes as I reversed and without noticing and not applying the brake! I reached forward to retrieve it. The wheelchair shot backwards into the passage and I went bump onto the floor of the bathroom. I then crawled on my knees to retrieve the wheelchair and pulled myself up on the edge of the bath to get back onto the seat of the chair. Boy was my "bum" sore and my pride hurt! No repercussions in my ankle after this embarrassing episode.

The 12th November, nearly halfway for my ankle being in plaster but I was struggling with the use of the strideon and finding it very difficult to mount the scooter. So much so, I rang the physiotherapist at the Nuffield to get advice. After explaining my difficulty, she asked a few questions and then realised my problem stemmed from having had an ankle fusion on my left ankle twenty years ago and there was no flexibility in making it easy to stand up on one leg. When I thought about it, this was the reason I had a bath lift installed twelve months ago. I would not, however, give up trying again in a few days! I was able to have a bath; the bath lift was an absolute help, I just slid across from my wheelchair and with the use of the limbo, and a waterproof leg cover I could be gently lowered into the water. It felt so much better after a refreshing bath. The physiotherapists told me that the date for plaster removal, x-ray and seeing the surgeon was 6th December. Then onto a boot for six weeks.

Over those last few days I had quite a severe headache which even paracetamol did not seem to help. So, one morning I phoned the surgery asking to speak with a doctor (after consulting with the Nuffield Hospital).

I was referred to the Witheridge surgery as ours was closed for ten days to upgrade. I actually saw my own doctor at 3.45 pm and after examination referred me to the Exeter hospital due to the blood thinning drug that I had self injected every day. This could in some cases cause a brain bleed and severe headache.

We arrived at the medical triage unit at 5.30 pm, booked in at a very busy area. No room in the waiting room so waited in the passage for two hours! Then called into the observation area for routine bloods, swabs, temperature and blood pressure. We waited until 10.45 pm when taken to a bed in the ward and after ten minutes was seen by a doctor. I was told I would need a CT scan and lumber puncture in the morning, so I was admitted at 11.15 pm. Six beds in B wing. A sleepless night due to blood pressure taken every two hours. Breakfast at 8 am and seen by the consultant at 9 am. He figured I should have a CT scan as a precaution in case of a brain bleed but did not think I needed a lumber puncture at this point. The Sister on the ward said it would be early in the day but it was in fact 12 midday! The scan probably took no more than five minutes and the results would be due in one to two hours. At 5.30 pm the result was good news – no bleed, headaches caused by my fall from the wheelchair, a week ago and I was discharged.

Daughter Wendy and Jan arrived at 6 pm and I was wheelchaired out of the hospital. Everything went well until crossing the road to the car park, when halfway across one of the rubber tyres (solid) came off the rim. We had to move out of the road quickly and a struggle for them to get me to the car.

After I scrambled in, horror ensued when Wendy lost her handbag. Jan rang her mobile numbers but no ringing in the vehicle! After a long search it was found folded up in the wheelchair! Home at 6.30–8pm to bed, I was quite exhausted but relieved to be home.

I would have to contact the Red Cross because the tyres on the chair were in quite a state but they did not open on a Wednesday in Sowton. We changed the chair on Thursday as I also had an appointment with the chiropractor on Friday to sort out the reason for my headaches. Neck problems were confirmed and put right. They advised me to have some laser treatment on my ankle when it was due to come out of plaster on 6th December. Another episode in this period was the toilet seat which became unstable due to a pin breaking. There had to be a simple solution – buy new plastic parts, but it took three visits for Jan to find what was necessary. It stated that these parts fit most loo seats. No they did not, when we got it home, so after drill and grinder I adapted them after couple of hours!

December 6th. The day of removal of plaster and fitting of boot. At hospital, short wait, when the surgeon took us into treatment room where he used a miniature "chainsaw" to cut the plaster, along the foot and up the leg. Then a calliper that split between the cut. The saw is a marvellous device because it does not cut or snip the skin at all. The four areas where the keyhole procedure of fitting two screws that locked the ankle boot together, were visible with no signs of blood! I was then x-rayed and two pictures were taken and sent to the consulting room screen. We were told everything looked good and we were then taken to the physiotherapy room for the fitting of a support boot which I would be in for six weeks. Then I saw the surgeon again and had a final x-ray. I could put some light weight on my foot in three weeks, then a trial run on a pair of crutches which went reasonably well. The results were good but it took time and a stick to walk up or down hill.

CHAPTER 8

DEVELOPMENT OF THE WOODLANDS AND CONSERVATION, 2010-2020

In our 82 acres of woodland the varieties of trees are now showing excellent growth rates (except for our ASH!). We have in our replanting areas introduced some other ones that were not there before. These included black walnut, wild sevice and hornbeam and believe it not, after some gentle persuasion 3 acres of Sitka spruce. I had for years only wanted to grow native broadleaves with just a few Scotch pine in groups of six or seven. One of the reasons was that behind Bickleigh Castle there were more than twenty acres of larch and other pine trees. During and after the 39/45 war I remembered this area was planted in mostly potatoes.

After Ash Dieback we had to get a ten-year Management Plan. The application form from the Forestry Commission was some 30 pages and I had a chance meeting with Chris Marrow who was a professional forestry consultant. I had known Chris when we were both Trustees of the Silvanus Trust and he helped me enormously with the paperwork and with first class advice. He, although it sounds posh, is my woodland manager with budgets and regular visits especially when Nick Downie is knee felling and thinning diseased ash. His contribution is invaluable in keeping the woods in good management.

Many years on now since 2015, we have removed a huge number of the Ash Dieback trees whilst creating better access to the overall woodland. Now remaining areas that are not accessible with the Harvester will have to be dealt with by hand and chainsaw.

People now admire the various autumn colours, with the wild cherry 'reds' the field maple yellows and the numerous berries on the path side shrubs, such as spindle, guelder rose, hawthorn, rowan, alder, buckthorn, holly and whortleberry and leaves add a combination of colours to our woodland glades.

Here at Byway, we have tried to create a mix of trees that people can enjoy for generations to come. The last ten years have seen our efforts in conservation develop and grow and enjoyed not just by ourselves but many people who walk our woodland and wildflower meadows. As you can see by the photographs there are many different trees and wildflowers year by year. I have kept a record since 2010 of things like the arrival of

Bluebell ramble.

swallows, the first brimstone butterfly, orange tip, the first wild daffodils, frog spawn in the ponds, the sound of the chiffchaff then the thrush, or the first snowdrop to herald spring. Being able to look down the river and across the Exe Valley it gives us such pleasure watching the birds at our feeders at all times of the year. We regularly see herons, kingfishers, yellow wagtails and dippers down by the river, with now the occasional little egret up and down the river whilst mallard Exmoor hen use our ponds at all times of the year. Even some rare birds have visits from time to time. This year we saw some stonechats down by our Dutch barn and a beautiful sight of a barn owl. What a sight to see buzzards that are here year by year, with one special one that carries a nearly white plumage. Birds that we now never see are greenfinch, yellow hammer, skylark or lapwings which I last saw here in 2010, nor have we heard the cuckoo since 2010.

Most of our ponds (as you can see in the pictures) have now wide varieties of water flowers from yellow flag, blue iris, marsh marigolds, cowslips, yellow and purple loosestrife and three or four types of water lilies. Otters visited the pond in 2016 and I managed to get sight of one with three young cubs on my movement camera.

Our Bluebell Walk in aid of the charity Children's Hospice South West (Little Bridge House in Barnstaple) is important and we try to keep going with the help of the Tiverton Committee. In 2018, for the first time in twenty-five years, we had to postpone it for two weeks because of the late spring. This year, 2020, the first bluebells in our wood were visible in early March, but sadly the walk was cancelled because of Covid-19.

Our wildflower area, below the bungalow, has been improving year by year with many cowslips, primroses, snowdrops, oxeye daisies, ragged robin, red champion, foxgloves and teasels amongst the apple and plum trees and some garden shrubs. The swallows, although fewer this year, regularly nest in our garage but we only see the occasional swift. We luckily see a huge variety of butterflies in summer and autumn including red admirals, peacock, marbled white, holly blue, skippers, meadow brown ringlets to name but a few.

In the woodland we do try to control the grey squirrels who can do so much damage to our young trees. We try to also keep the number of magpies from decimating our young songbird population. Spotted woodpeckers visit out feeders and seem to disappear in July and August. The green woodpecker is conspicuous by its call and my father called it the WET, WET BIRD at which he said we should not try to make hay as it is a sign of rain in the air! They feed mostly on ants and our Great Hill steep is eroded by many ant hills some as high as 2 feet. What a marvellous achievement to build them: it must be like building a mountain for such small creatures.

How lucky we are in this lockdown period to be able to enjoy the sounds and sights of nature in the Exe Valley here in Devon.

Bluebell, by Chloe.

Wild Flowers on Byway – Flowers on Dry Land

A Agrimony
Angelica

B Bird's Foot Trefoil
Bluebell
Buttercup
Broom
Burdock
Bindweed
Betony
Bugle
Black Medic

C Celandine
Crone's bill
Charlock
Campion (Red & White)
Cow Parsley
Cuckoo Flower
Corn Cockie
Corn Flower
Colts Foot
Common Centuary
Clover(Red & White)
Comfrey
Creeping Cinquefoil
Common Mouse Ear
Chickory

D Dog Rose
Devils Bit Scabious
Dandelion
Daisy
Dead Nettle
Daffodill (Wild)

E Eyebright

F Field rose
Flax
Foxglove
Fat Hen
Forget Me Not
Fleabane
Field Gentian
Fennel
Fox & Cubs

G Gorse
Golden Rod
Greater Willow Herb
Garlic Mustard
Greater Plantain
Groundsel
Goats Beard
Greater Bird's Foot Trefoil

H Hogsweed
Hedge Mustard
Hedge Bindweed
Hawks Bit
Honeysuckle
Hemp Nettle
Haws Beard

I Ivy (Ground)

K Knap Weed

L Lords and Ladies
Ladies Bedstraw
Lesser Trefoil

M Meadow Buttercup
Mullen Great
Musk Mallow &
Common
May Weed
Milk Maid
Meadow Verwling
Melancholy Thistle

N Navel Wort
Nipple Wort

O Ox-Eye Daisy
Orchid Common
Spotted Orchid
Early Purple

P Penny Wort
Periwinkle
Pignut
Primose
Poppy
Pansy (Wild)
Pink Purslane

R Ragged Robin
Ramsons
Rosebay Willow Herb
Red Shank
Ribwort
Red Clover

S   Scarlet Pimpernel

Speedwell

Silver Weed

Sorrel

Snakes Head Fritillary

Shepherd's Purse

St John's Wort

Stitch Wort (Greater & Lesser)

Strawberry (Wild)

Salad Burnet

Star of Bethlehem

Self Heal

Spurge

Solomon's Seal

Spear Thistle

Scabious

Sneeze Wort

T   Three Cornered Leek

Toadflax

Teasel

Tormentil

V   Vetch (common & tufted)

Valerian

Violet (Dog)

W   Wood Sorrel

Wood Spurge

Wood Anemone

Wood Wort

Wild Carrot

Willowherb

Y   Yarrow

Yellow Rattle

Yellow Archangel

Orchid spread.

Wild Flowers on Byway – Flowers on Wet Land

A	Arrow Head	**S**	Sweet Flag
B	Bistort	**W**	Water Violet
	Bog Bean		Water Forget Me Not
	Brocklime		Water Plantain
	Bulrush		Water Lilies-
	Bedstraw		Yellow
	Bog Asphodel		White
C	Cowslip		Pink
I	Indian Balsam		Water Cress
	Iris (Blue)		Water Mint
L	Lesser Spearwort		Water Crowfoot
	Loosestrife (purple)		Water Soldier
	Loosestrife (Yellow)		Wood Anemone
	Ladies Smock		Water Aven
M	Meadow Sweet	**Y**	Yellow Flag Iris
	Marsh Marigold		
O	Orchid		
	Southern Marsh		
	Heath spotted		
	Common		
P	Pickerell Weed		

Heath spotted orchid.

Trees and Shrubs on Byway Farm

	Trees	Shrubs
A	Ash, Aspen, Alder	Alder, Buckthorn
B	Beech, Birch, Silver & Downy	Blackthorn Buddleia
C	Wild Cherry, Sweet Chestnut, Horse Chestnut	Crab Apple
D		Dogwood
E	Eucalyptus White Elm Elder	English Elm
F	Field Maple	
G		Guelder Rose Grey Willow
H	Hornbeam	Hawthorn Hazel, Holly, Honeysuckle
I		Ivy
L	Small Leaved Lime	Liquidambar
O	Oak (Sessile, Pedunculate, Red)	
P	Paperback Maple	
R	Rowan	
S	Sycamore Scotch Pine Sikta Spruce	Strawberry Tree Spindle
T	Tulip Tree	
W	Wych Elm Wayfarer Walnut & Black Wild Service	

Butterflies Regularly Seen

Peacock, Red Admiral, Brimstone,
Small Tortoiseshell, Painted Lady, Orange Tip, Holly
Blue, Speckled Wood, Large White, Ringlet, Small
Copper, Skipper, Painted Lady,
Comma Gatekeeper, Meadow Brown,
Marbled White, Brown Hairstreak

Birds Seen at Byway in the Last Ten Years

Barn Owl	Greenfinch	Robin
Black Cap	Grey Heron	Rook
Blackbird	Gulls	Snipe
Blue Tit	House Martin	Song Thrush
Bullfinch	House Sparrow	Sparrow Hawk
Buzzard	Jackdaw	Starling
Chaffinch	Jay	Stonechat
Chiffchaff	Kestrel	Swallow
Coal Tit	Kingfisher	Swan
Coot	Little Egret	Swift
Cormorant	Longtail Tit	Tawny Owl
Crow	Magpie	Teal
Dipper	Mallard	Wagtail Grey Pied
Dove Collared	Mistle Thrush	Wood Pigeon
Dove Stock	Moorhen	Woodcock
Dunnock	Nuthatch	Woodpecker Green
Feral Pigeon	Pheasant	Woodpecker Spotted
Field Fare	Pied Wagtail	Wren
Flycatcher	Raven	Wryneck
Goldfinch	Red Wing	

Country Sayings

- East wind blowing in the winter brings snow
- Oak leaves, out before ash, a splash for summer
- Ash before oak, a soak for the summer
- 13 new moons in a year, does not bode well for good summer weather
- Rain before 7 usually stops before 11
- Farmers usually keep an eye on the barometer, or hang up some seaweed outside the backdoor!
- A swarm of bees in May is worth a load of hay
- A swarm of bees in June is worth a silver spoon
- A swarm of bees in July is not worth a fly
- If March comes in like a LION it will go out like a LAMB
- If March comes in like a LAMB it will go out like a LION
- Cast not a clout until May is out
- Cut dashels (thistles) in May they will come next day
- Cut dashels (thistles) in June they will come again soon
- Cut dashels (thistles) in July they are sure to die!
- Don't wash a blanket in May – t'will wash a member of family away
- Fog on the hill brings water to the mill
- If Candlemas Day be fair and bright – winter will have another fight
- If Candlemas Day be a dull day – winter's over for another year
- If it does not rain on St Swithin's Day, 40 days dry
- If it does rain on St Swithin's Day, 40 days of rain
- Franklands Day May 19th-21st – Don't put flowers or vegetables in the outside as frost is still possible till those dates

Collective Names of Birds

Fall of Woodock, Deceit of Lapwings, Parliament of Rooks, Unkindness of Ravens, Congregation of Plovers, Herd of Wrens, Covey of Partridges, Tiding of Magpies, Exaltation or Bevy of Larks, Murmuration of Starlings and a Charm of Goldfinches

Carrot flower.

FARMER JOHN'S LAMENT

*When I took up farming I was just a lad. I looked at our pastures and my
heart was glad.*

*I was ready to take on the world if need be, and a good fruitful future was
all I could see.*

*Then a man from the Ministry came to my door and said "Now young
fellow, you must produce more.*

*In London we've worked out a wonderful plan to double your output, make
you a rich man."*

"Half your land is just hedge and wood. How can that possibly be any good?

*Improve your acres and efficiency and I will make sure that you're paid
handsomely."*

*So I followed his schemes, although it was hard when the last of the horses
went from our yard.*

*I bought a new tractor and a big Ransomes plough; it brings me to tears
when I think of it now.*

*We ploughed up the scrublands, orchids and all, and with great satisfaction
watched the trees fall.*

*We burnt up the branches and blew out the stumps – the ponds in the
meadow were our rubbish dumps.*

*We grubbed out the hedges to make larger fields, the bigger the better, to
increase our yields.*

*We worked on like beavers and never once paused, and were paid very well
for the havoc we caused.*

Forty years on there's a knock on the door. The man from the Ministry, same as before.

"There's cash to make now if you plant a tree. It's awfully exciting I think you'll agree.

We'd rather like some of your farm to grow wild just like you remember when you were a child;

A hedge by the hillside, a copse just beyond while for fishes and frogs a nice stream and pond."

Well. Now I'm newly retired and I sing this sad song. Some of the things I did were so wrong.

"What did the most damage?" I ask constantly. "The man from the Ministry, Dutch elm, Ash Dieback, OR ME !"

Dormouse.

Lady's smock trail.

Outside the palace with my MBE.

In the orchard.

Bee on bistort.

Garden view.

Apples ready to be picked.

Burnet moth.

Autumn berries – guelder rose.

Coming in to land.

Bee in blue iris.

Devil's bit.

82

Dragonfly detail.

Moth on pickerell weed.

Yarrow.

83

Pond in bloom.

White water lily.

Stunning red rowan berries.

A carpet of bluebells.

Cornflower.

Southern marsh orchid.

Melancholy thistle.

Guelder rose.

Wood anenome.

Woodland Path.

Yellow flag.

Living beech trees.

Chicory.

Bird's foot trefoil.

Bluebells in the wood.

CHAPTER 9

BBC RADIO DEVON, THE MID DEVON MESSENGER AND MORE SIGNIFICANT MEMORIES

Radio Devon

Some two years ago, when my friend Pippa Quelch was moved from a Sunday morning slot on Radio Devon to late afternoon weekdays, we took the decision for me to retire from my Farmer John monthly chat about life on the farm and conservation with the talented broadcaster Pippa. Then in came Covid-19 and she was on the air every other week between 10–2pm. Lo and behold, came a telephone call asking if I could talk with her on the radio, about times past and present on the farm once a month. So, I have talked about life during and after World War II and comparing life with now and then. I also did another slot about shearing and dipping in years gone past.

Mid Devon Messenger

Just over twelve months ago I was asked by a neighbour, Rose, if I would be interested in doing a twelve-minute slot with her, for the people in Mid Devon who have little or no sight (Mid Devon Messenger). It seemed a good thing for me to do, as someone who has permanent eye problems. The feedback has so far been very good, as we sometimes record in woodland, ponds, or wildflower meadows.

Pippa Quelch helping with some planting.

Recording for the Mid Devon Messenger.

Invaders

Just before Christmas 2019 we had a shock one morning, when an area of lawn was turned upside down and on investigation, we found footprints that were later identified as coming from wild boar, so locals be warned!

Shearing

In January 2020, I took the decision to retire, after forty years, as a scorer of sheep shearing competitions in the South West England. There comes a time in life when difficult decisions have to be made, as my eyesight has deteriorated in the last twelve months. I have a leaking vein behind my right eye, so I need an injection every two months in the back of my eye. The condition cannot be cured but, hopefully the treatment will stop me from losing my eyesight. I shall miss all my friends, shearers, judges and stewards who I have worked with over a long period of time, enjoying the banter as a team.

Solar Panels

In January 2012, we employed a local firm to install solar panels on our garage roof. We had been let down, prior to Christmas, by an upcountry firm, full of promises to have them up and running before a drop in government subsidies per kilowatt produced. They did not fulfil their promise! There was a national appeal to extend the full subsidy which was successful so the local firm, although a little dearer, were employed for the installation. This firm is still in business today whereas the other went bankrupt! We were lucky to receive the full subsidy from day one and by 2019 they had paid back the initial investment. This year has seen a great return after all the amount of sunshine in April and May. With the solar panels plus our eighty acres of woodland we have made a contribution towards reducing global warming.

Bickleigh Garden Club

In 2015 I was persuaded to become Chairman of this club, of which I had been the Treasurer for the previous three years. Those who know me (especially the wife) also know that my knowledge of garden flowers is

Did we have wild boar in the night?

very limited. I cannot be let loose in the garden, so my job is usually is to dig holes for shrubs and take away the rubbish! Our club has about forty members coming from neighbouring villages. It becomes increasingly more difficult, these days, to find people to take an office and I hear this in many organisations. Each year we hold a spring sale of shrubs and plants and a show in August where our entries have received many compliments over the years. We are proud that one of our members is 101 YEARS YOUNG and enters floral entries every year, as well as attending most of our meetings!

Tiverton Agriculture Association Trustees

In 2014 I gave up the Chair after several years of working with an excellent group of Trustees who meet twice a year, giving financial support to young people needing support travelling, garden clubs within our area, and ploughing associations to name some of our rural interests. My good friend Roger Hill has taken on the role with more enthusiasm continuing the good work of the Trust.

Metal Detecting

In the last ten years we have been visited by Rex from Tiverton whose hobby in retirement was Metal Detecting and on his first visit I was quite sceptical that he would find anything of interest. How wrong was I. He was extremely tidy when finding metal objects under the ground; he would always replace the turf after a find. He found many coins which included a Longshanks Edward 1st dated 1239-1307, another James the First shilling and a heap of Victorian ones plus buckles and a medal in good condition. A group from East Devon found four post medieval coins in one spot in the orchard. They were treated as treasure trove because it was more than two! After an inquest they were given to the Royal Albert Museum for public benefit. I must thank him for all the finds, he was insistent that we keep them. He has now moved away to the Midlands to be with his brother. What a shame! I was hoping he would have found that POT OF GOLD!

Water Troubles

In 1972 we had the opportunity to bring mains water down through the farm. Mr Britton was contracted to lay the water pipe from the end of Prowse's Lane, installing water troughs in every field on the route. The lane is on the Crediton road, up the lane for half a mile, then down through another one mile of fields, fitting the troughs, as necessary. Eventually it reached our cattle sheds after using the old black pipe (now green). As time went by we connected it to the farmhouse and an adjoining barn which we had sold to a local vet for conversion to holiday lets. This led to a change in our farming policy, after a serious outbreak of TB, when we began our tree planting here on the hilly land first, then to become nearly 80 acres.

All went well until 2017-18 when we developed two major leaks which cost us quite a lot of money! Remember, our water meter is some 2 miles from our house, and in 2018 we found a leak had found its way into a stone drain around our cattle shed, so was not obvious above ground. This lesson brought us quickly into the 21st century when, on advice from SW Water a logger was fitted to the meter so we could check daily for major leaks. In 2019 we spotted a leak on the logger and after three days with digger driver Richard we realised, after a while it was going to be cheaper to put in 300 meters of new green pipe, as the original pipe was going through a good bit of woodland. We did put in several stop cocks on the route to be able to more easily find any future problems. The logger does cost us £250 a year but it will save us time and effort in the long run.

Other events

Jan and I have given up time to be participants in the Peninsula Medical School trials in Exeter over the last few years. I have been type 2 diabetic and they have been doing several tests for sufferers with this condition. Especially at this time, with Covid-19, I applaud all the NHS staff working in the wider community, with all this virus can throw at them. There are some very qualified people working hard to find a vaccine.

In this year the Greenslade family had been farming here for 100 years with three generations. Like everything in life, the farm has diversified in different ways. When grandfather came here, as a tenant under the Fursdon Estate at Cadbury, my father was only seven and when he grew up there were no agriculture colleges, no computers, and no tractors. He learnt his skills from his father. When I left school I had the benefit of being a member of Withleigh Young Farmers Club where I attended courses in hedging, milking, machinery maintenance, etc. I was proud to attain a gold proficiency badge for passing seven selected tests. I owe a great debt of gratitude to the YFC movement for my achievements in life and I am very proud to be an Honorary Life Vice-President of Devon YFC.

CHAPTER 10

SOME POETRY FROM MY SISTER MARGARET

Happy Birthday Brother!

*I find it hard to believe your age,
it's such a great number!
Born in 1940 – it must be right –
But I just can't write it on the page!*

*As a young man, you were a busy young farmer,
And running Way Farm with Dad
With Jan, his wife and 3 daughters –
What a busy life you had!*

*With the girls left home and settled,
Along came grandchildren – six!
Three handsome boys and three pretty girls
To add to the family mix*

*As mid-life beckoned, never bored,
Magistrates, Woodland Trust, while all alone on local Radio Devon,
Each week, FARMER JOHN!*

*Then retirement beckoned sheep shearing judging at all the shows,
And talk to lots of evening groups
To keep you on your toes!*

*No-one can say your life's been boring
You've overfilled each minute –
Now at your great age, relax a bit
If you've a clue how to do it!!
Have a great birthday xx*

My sister Margaret and me

Autumn Creatures

In these shortening days of autumn, we've had a mass migration

And although completely harmless, they are a source of irritation

While walking the dogs with every step, like phantoms from the ground

They are rising up and flying off to our house I'll be bound

When it gets dark, with curtains pulled, they start making an appearance

My hubby says "They are here again" my job's to effect their clearance!

I know they are harmless creatures, they never sting or bite

But they really drive me crackers, when they are in the house at night

They love it in the lampshade, and prefer to be up high

So I take my life in both my hands, and wish that I could fly!

There are at least ten to be disposed of, in the lounge each night

Then when we get upstairs to bed, and turn on the bedside light

They appear from almost nowhere, sometimes over our head

And sometimes on the ceiling while I stretch up, teetering on the bed!

My hubby says "Just let them go", but I need to be realistic

Cos if one touched my face in the night, I am likely to go Ballistic!

Anyway I'd like to know, where did they get their name?

Long legs is understandable, but "DADDY", WHO IS TO BLAME

For making them all male by name, a strange idea – but lummy

It does not seem very fair To EVERY LONG-LEG MUMMY!

Covid-19 Poem

*Winter 2019/20 was horribly wet according to
records, the wettest one yet*

But worse was to come, started in the East

In Wuhan, in China a virus a beast

*At the time it seemed unbelievable that from a
Chinese market, it came from a bat*

It started as an epidemic quite fast it spread

*Respiratory symptoms leaving
sufferers dead*

It spread very quickly to Italy and Spain

Carried, no doubt, by travellers by plane

*Symptoms were high temperature and
a cough*

That's persistent and hard to fight off

Respiratory problems filled up ICU

The need for more beds grew and grew

Nightingale Hospitals were built very quick

*To accommodate increasing numbers
of sick*

Each day the death toll was alarming high

*Even Boris got it and was feared he
may die*

Only the news seemed to get worse

But each Thursday at 8, we'd clap for each doctor and nurse

23rd March we were put under lockdown, Hotels, cafés & shops had to shut down

Life for all became unreal

Stay indoors, stay safe & save the NHS was the deal

It was all new – furloughed workers

Home schooling and social distancing to keep

Grants to help struggling businesses

On-line shopping with delivery fairly cheap

Now the lockdown is easing

But everyone's nervous

And anxious to take chances

To resume normal service

There's lots of walking

And folk on their bike

Heaven preserve us from

The threatened second spike!

My Brother John – A Tribute

I can't believe he's really gone.
That lovely man – my brother John.
For all the family such a shock.
Cos for all of us – he's been our rock.

With words of wisdom always there.
All our joys and griefs to share.
A one-off superstar in his life.
To grandchildren, daughters, sister and wife.

Him and I were brought up at Way.
From a very young age, helping make hay.
A shining example to us both – Mum and Dad.
Unconditional love was what we had.

John loved farming – preferred it to school.
Dodging teacher thrown board rubbers as a rule!!
Passed the 11+, Tivvy Grammar school bound,
Before and after school, working on the farm he could be found.

In those days our social life was nil,
But luckily the Young Farmers Club was there that space to fill.
We learnt a lot at Withleigh YFC.
Being five years older, he always looked out for me.

Once he could drive, he was out and free.
Classes and dances with the YFC.
He met Janette, and he was smitten.
Their life together was then written.

Wed in Cullompton in April '64
The Rectory Flat at Bickleigh – they had the key of the door.
A few years later, dad built the bungalow at Way.
So John was on the spot, to help every single day.

Then the girls arrived – 1, 2 and 3
Ensuring continuity of the Family Tree!
Sally, Wendy and Julie, of his girls he was proud.
Completing his family, a pat on the back allowed.

So by now, apart from his family and farming at Way.
There were other jobs that he had picked up on the way!
Founder member of Mid-Devon Show,
And chairman of Devon YFC – ones I know!

Also many years on the bench as a respected JP.
No chance of ever getting bored you can see!
Recently he worked with the partially- sighted,
With eye problems himself, he was more than delighted.

All the while, planting his much-loved woodland,
And wild flower meadows and ponds to enjoy and
Then encouraging visitors, Bluebell walks too,
Raising money for deserving causes, it's true.

As a result of all this, his proudest moment came to be,
When he was deservedly awarded an MBE.
Our parents would have burst with pride,
Of all his achievements it can't be denied.

To date, 3 daughters, six grandchildren too,
But also 5 great-grandchildren in the family crew.
John was rightly proud of each and every one.
And they of him, and all in his life he had done.

Oh – and Farmer John contributed to Radio Devon for 20 years,
His voice was well-known to regular's ears!
He published one book – and just finished another.
'Twas a proper Job' – in the words of my Brother.

I miss you John, Love Marg xx

CHAPTER 11

FAMILY AND LOST FRIENDS

Family should come first, and in my case it does! We are lucky to have such a diverse and loving family to be so proud of. Since 2010 two of my six grandchildren have married and now have families. Steven and Kirsty have two sweet girls, Roseanne and Charlotte, with the recent addition of twin boys William and Edward, the first in my side of the family for many a year! We have been able to see them on several occasions and they are two bonny babies.

Laura and Mike have an agriculture business and a flock of poll Dorset sheep and have a bonny boy, Robert who is twelve months old. Richard and Sally have a large herd of Canadian Holstein Friesian cattle milking about 250 cows. They won two trophies last year, the best Family Farm and the Best Dairy Farm in the South West. What an achievement, with son Steven taking a leading role in the breeding where he uses sexed semen, embryo transplant which is the modern way today. They now farm my river meadows, in either grass or maize silage.

Daughter Wendy works for Somerset County Council dealing with schooling matters, while Keith runs his own gas business in Wellington. Their son Alex, who helped me to compile my first book, now lives in Toronto, Canada and became engaged to his love Emma last Christmas, with marriage next year. He has done well in Canada, working in finance for RBC as a financial advisor, becoming an associate in his division. He has started a Masters in Tax Law and has passed the Bar exam and wishing to become a tax lawyer. The future looks bright for him! His sister Jess is a qualified health professional at the RD Exeter Hospital and has recently bought her first home close to the Hospital. I often tease her saying "Can

With my wife, Janette and daughters.

you marry a doctor; we need one in the Family as we get older". We could do with some help in our old age! She is one of the NHS HEROES working through the Covid-19 Pandemic.

Youngest daughter Julie lives in Roscommon, Southern Ireland, where she lives with her children Abbie aged twelve and Arley aged eight, so they are considerably younger than our other grandchildren. She works part time for the Dogs Trust, but has a busy dog grooming business. We have flown on many occasions to Knock Airport, hired a car for an hour's drive away, where we meet the wonderful hospitality of the Irish people. She has lived in Ireland for more than twenty-four years but has not acquired the Irish accent unlike her two children! We were to meet up on my eightieth birthday in March but Covid-19 scuppered all those plans!

My brother in law John Leach had a leading role as sales manager when the German tractors came to the UK some years ago. He had previously sold tractors for several businesses in Devon and Dorset. When the Deutz came over to UK he found dealerships throughout the country but after a few years he left to take up a similar position with Fendt Tractors. Many contractors use these well-made ones with good reliability and construction. He sold us one twenty-five years ago which I still use regularly, so like me, we are both vintage!

Grandchildren.

My sister, Margaret still lives in Weymouth where she is a part-time registrar (and still working well past the normal retirement age) and one of her granddaughters has now become a full time registrar in Dorset.

In 2014 we received sad news that my cousin, Barry Greenslade had died of a heart attack aged seventy-four in Portage La Prairie Canada. I have to thank my sister and daughter for tracing family history some years previously when we became reunited with part of our long lost family. We had stayed with them in 2004 while they had come to Devon to visit his grandfather's old homes in Witheridge where he was a cobbler. We are still in contact with his family which is a part of my life story!

In 2017 my very good friend, Arthur Rundle developed lung cancer. He was a true Cornishman – you know, jam first on a scone, then the cream, the other way in Devon. We had worked together at many South West shows doing the scoring for Shearing competitions for over twenty years, me doing the mental work and he putting the judge scores into the laptop programme. We had known each other a long time. I was the County Chairman of Devon Young Farmers in 1966, he held the same position in Cornwall. In 1992 Wesley Wilton was the chief steward at the Royal Bath and West Show World Shearing competitions and I was invited to help with the event. Following a successful event, I was persuaded to help with the scoring annually, and when Arthur become chief steward we worked together until his death in December. He had been secretary of the World Council after Wesley Wilton as well as chief steward at Bath and West for a good number of years. We were invited to the World championship in Norway when it was held there which was a fantastic country to visit. We last worked together at the famous Widdecombe Fair in September but were honoured to be part of his family at his funeral at Stoke Climsland church. We still miss his Cornish voice but we keep in touch with his sister Margaret in Gunnislake.

In 2020 I have lost very good friends. Albert Cook from Filleigh in North Devon, who I knew well, as we had judged many YFC competitions together in years past. Over many occasions he had tried to persuade me

Meeting up with great grandchildren after lockdown.

Robert, great grandson.

to become a magistrate and until I gave up the dairy herd in 1988 I had resisted. Soon after the sale he encouraged me to let him put my name forward for an interview. I was appointed to the Cullompton Bench and then followed 20 years of once a fortnight sittings there and Heavitree court in Exeter until I was nearly seventy years old.

I have also worked with him in the shearing world where he had been a champion shearer and a well-respected judge. We met on several occasions at various events, usually trying to put the "World to rights"! When he became the President of Devon County Show it was a special day for both of us, when he presented the Watkins Trophy which we won in the Woodland Competition for the fourth time. Although 95 years old he kept a keen interest in the Farming World especially in his beloved Devon Closewool Sheep.

The following month we had the shock news that our good friend John Daw had died suddenly. We had been in YFC and judged many competitions together over the years. He and his wife Marilyn were there at the very first Mid Devon Show with Marilyn, our first secretary, and John a livestock steward for the first three years. At his funeral at Crediton church there was standing room only as a tribute for all work as a farmer, a former Chairman of Mid Devon District Council, member and commentator at Mid Devon Show amongst other activities. At show meetings he was usually late, but he could talk his way out of a "traffic jam". After an operation, Jan and I were not fit enough to lamb some young Poll Dorset ewes so he bought them saving us all the hassle. Again Devon has lost a TRUE MAN OF THE SOIL.

In May this year we lost a very good friend who had a considerable influence on our conservation projects here on the farm. I had been friends with the Cole family for many a long year but Cyril's gift of dowsing whether it be for boreholes or for ponds was legendary, having dowsed over seven hundred over the South West with brilliant accuracy. He dowsed a borehole for our bungalow as well as six ponds which has saved us hundreds of pounds in water charges. After seeing his wildflower meadows, we were inspired to create some ourselves and his advice and help has been invaluable. His love of barn owls was a thing we both shared and he built three nest boxes which he erected here on the farm which have been used by the lovely birds on several occasions. He had textbook knowledge of birds and wildflowers of every kind. We had sighting of an unusual bird this spring, but after a call to Cyril he soon identified it as a stonechat, which I have not seen here before. He hosted many visitors to their farm and one amusing thing we overheard that we were the FLOWERING WEED FARMERS!

Thank you, Cyril, for your contribution to conservation in the West Country.

I have lost another dear friend who rode on the back of my quad bike all around the farm. Where I went she was always with me. My spaniel Bella was fifteen years old and during the last two months developed a serious internal problem from which she could not recover, so sadly we had to let the local vet put her to sleep. Those of you who came on our walks would be met with a "waggly tail" and she would always go with us around the farm. We miss her like one of the FAMILY.

Bella.

CHAPTER 12

'TIS A PROPER JOB!

A s my life goes on, despite a few medical problems along the way, I am in reasonable health to be able to continue our enjoyment of developing further our farm. Hoping that in future others might appreciate our efforts in preserving our Woodlands and Wildflower Meadows here in the Exe Valley. I feel privileged to have lived through the horse era, the steel wheel tractor, the now more modern tractor with satellite guidance and all the more advanced machinery. I have milked cows by hand, then by machine bucket, then six at a time in a parlour (now many more than this on some farms), now there are many Robots

Leading the Bluebell Walk.

Knapweed paradise.

where the cows organize their own milking without human intervention! Never did I think I would see this in my lifetime and wonder what more advances there will be in the next ten years. I do worry about the amount of land being taken for solar panels; surely, they could be installed on the numerous industrial buildings in the cities. The erection of anaerobic digesters is taking many acres of land to feed them which is surely needed to grow food for the UK so we do not need so much imported food.

So far my life has been a great adventure. I remember the advice I was given when I joined the Withleigh Young Farmers Club, many years ago "Whatever you do in the Club or life, try to leave it better than when joined it".

The book is dedicated to my many family and friends (past and present) who have helped me to farm and enjoy whatever I have been involved in over the last eighty years.

'TIS BEEN A PROPER JOB!

CHAPTER 13

EUOLOGY

Ladies and Gentleman, we are gathered here today to pay tribute to a true Gentleman. His ability to communicate with people of all ages, backgrounds and beliefs coupled with his love and understanding of the countryside and all its wonders, touched the lives of so many.

His wisdom, intellect, warmth and genuine ability to help others will be etched in our memories for ever. I realised as our friendship developed that his loyalty first and foremost was to his family. I would like to say a huge thank you on their behalf for all the kind messages of support which just proves the high esteem in which John was regarded.

To me he was my mentor, a guiding light, great companion and the very best of friends. When he took me under his wing many years ago, he gave me some advice that has forever remained with me. "Roger", he said, "Life is not a dress rehearsal."

He certainly lived up to his philosophy. Farmer John, as he was affectionately known, was a Farmer first but soon became a passionate YFC supporter, a Countryman, public speaker, showman, competition judge, sportsman, radio personality, magistrate, fundraiser and much, much, more.

Life was tough when he was born on 15th March 1940. It was war with blackouts, the threat of bombs, no electricity or mains water and rationing. It did not help because he was a fussy eater. His mother was told. "You will never rear thicky one."

One bright aspect was whereas most people only had one loo, the Greenslade family had two. Both unfortunately were outside.

School began at Tiverton Primary, but to get there he had to ride a bike across fields to Burn Holt to catch a train. After passing his eleven plus he attended Tiverton Grammar School where he excelled especially at sport. How he had enough energy though, because on top of the journey he had helped milk the cows before he set off in the morning.

His one ambition was to come home and work on the farm, which he realised in 1956. Never afraid of hard work, he increased the number of cattle and sheep, started rearing turkeys and did contract work for neighbouring farmers.

Just as most young lads he persuaded his dad to modernise by purchasing a little Grey Fergie to complement the horses and the introduction of mains electric in 1960 accelerated the process. Over the years John became a peer amongst his fellow farmers culminating in being invited to judge at many events.

In all that he had achieved there was one that would change his life for ever. Joining Withleigh YFC on leaving school its motto was "Good Farmers, Good Countrymen, Good Citizens". He quickly fulfilled all three.

The youth movement soon lived up to its reputation as a marriage bureau because in 1959 he met Janette at a Whimple dance. They became engaged at Christmas 1962 but unfortunately on Boxing Day it began snowing for six weeks and they could not meet up. No mobile phones, Skype or Zoom in those days.

They married in 1964 and began life together in the Rectory Flat at Bickleigh. Four years later they moved back to Way Farm having had a bungalow built. Three daughters arrived. Sally, Wendy and Julie. Since then, the family has expanded with six grandchildren and five great grandchildren.

With Janette's backing he partook in a whole range of YFC skills and went on to teach hundreds of young people. He became an adept public speaker. Winning numerous awards culminated in a travel scholarship to Denmark. Amongst many officer roles he became Chairman of Devon in 1966 and has been awarded honorary positions ever since.

Never afraid to do whatever it takes to raise money for charity, he joined me on an exhausting pram push dressed in a fluorescent wig, ample bosom and miniskirt. The responding wolf whistles made it all worthwhile.

Friendships in YFC last a lifetime and so it was that he invited me to join him as a steward for the sheep shearing at the Devon County Show. "We have to add up the points," he told me, "fingers and thumbs are allowed." We met Royalty and even celebrities like Noel Edmonds or was it Mr Blobby?

One day, after heavy rain outside our marquee John turned to me and asked, "Rog, are your feet getting wet?" A stream of water rushed beneath us carrying the newly shorn wool with it. During this time together I bounced an idea of starting an agricultural show in Mid Devon. I knew he would soon tell me if I was completely crazy but straight away he embraced the idea and helped drive the creation of Mid Devon Show forward. He and Jan worked tirelessly, and John became Show Director, Trade Stand Chairman and then President in 2013.

Not content he expanded his stewarding duties to the Royal Cornwall Show, Bath and West and even the World Championship in Norway.

He was appointed a Magistrate and served as a JP for twenty years. He became a Trustee and subsequent Chairman of the Tiverton Agricultural Association and also a Trustee of Silvanus Woodland.

The latter was a result of winning many prestigious awards after planting over 30 hectares of trees encouraging wildlife, flowers and fauna at the same time. It led to raising thousands of pounds for charity with the Bluebell Walks and education.

All this led to an invite to tell his story on Radio Devon in 1997. His contributions continued with a regular spot as Farmer John.

I knew he loved cricket, so I recruited him to our village team 'the Cavaliers.' We also travelled together to Taunton to watch Somerset where Ian Botham peppered the opposition's team bus in the car park. We all cheered when one ball went through the window. John later accompanied Ian Botham on one of his walks raising money for leukaemia.

It was on such cricketing occasions that I realised how much John loved ice cream. So, after a long day it wasn't a pint or a glass of wine, but a good old Devonshire vanilla.

With such a varied and interesting life, he wrote a book of his memoirs entitled *'Twas a Proper Job*. A second book has just been completed. To cap it all in 2017 he was awarded an MBE.

I am breathless with all his achievements having barely scratched the surface. All of you will have additional memories of a once in a generation gentleman.

We have all been privileged to have shared his company. We shall miss him terribly but we must stay positive as he would have wished and to leave this world, as he did, a better place for his contribution.

'Twas a proper job

Written by Roger Hill and read at Farmer John's funeral.